the volcano sequence

PITT POETRY SERIES

Ed Ochester, Editor

the volcano sequence

~ Alicia Suskin Ostriker

UNIVERSITY OF PITTSBURGH PRESS

The publication of this book
is supported by a grant from
the Pennsylvania Council on
the Arts

Published by the University of Pittsburgh Press,
Pittsburgh, Pa. 15260

Manufactured in the United States of America

Printed on acid-free paper

10 9 8 7 6 5 4 3 2 1

ISBN 0-8229-5784-1

for Anne Walsh

Lead me from the unreal to the real.

—Upanishads

There is nothing but what is said. Beyond what is said, there is nothing.

—Samuel Beckett

An ear, disjointed, eavesdrops.

—Paul Celan

Only in the space of this dialogue does that which is addressed take form and gather around the I who is addressing it.

—Paul Celan

contents

ruthless radiance

We are incapable of progressing vertically. We
cannot take a step toward the heavens.

—Simone Weil

1. volcano

Let me speak it to you in a whisper
I am like a volcano
that has blown itself
out of the water

my long stony curve
my melancholiac cliffs
a strip of old hard
exoskeleton

the blue Aegean flows
in and out of me
the tourists come, oh they come
to stand where the lava flew

to imagine how
the earth roared showed teeth
bucked and heaved
to look for an hour

at where the tidal wave began
that destroyed Atlantis
and created a myth
a green good world

you remember

~

A woman looked at my poem. What is a volcano? She wanted to know. What makes you like a volcano? What would the world be like without the myth of Atlantis?

the volcano is a crack in the earth
the volcano is a bulge over a crack
a fault line runs under it

something terrible happens
and the magma
coughs out

hot beauty
thick and magnificent rage
so what if afterward

everything is dead

~

when I was a child
I was an island
a small round bushy island
inside me were many

roots, rocks, ores,
flowings and crevasses wrinkled
pushing like joy, like fear's thin
fluids, like love's neediness

maybe too much
and somehow they all turned
to anger and for years
the lava poured and poured

righteously
destroying all
in its path
righteously

roaring

~

the myth of Atlantis lets us believe
the world used to be better

people lived in harmony and grace once
fish came asking to be caught

the moon shimmered like a mist
in the hair of women

and because we believe this
we have to blame someone   we have to

step down those slimy stairs

~

finally the lava stopped boiling
it cooled and hardened into what you see
blisters and carbuncles of cinders
rough and dry as the moon

striking terror, mindless
as an army, now it's quiet
except for a fringe of surf
and the sway of water in the crater

~

what is Atlantis
what is the myth of innocence
before and after the kick of time

oh amniotic worm
poor lentil wearing your archaic smile
soft baby rockabye

soon you'll be naked
rock cutting your tender feet
mud and tears coursing down your cheeks

the smell of money like brine
flags and bombs bursting around you
greed like a spirochete eating in

but if there is no Atlantis
no managed dream
how can a person breathe in that nihil air

doomed either way, dear God

2. the unmasking

I have come to sow the seed of light in the world
To unmask the God who disguises Himself as world

—Abraham Joshua Heschel

kh'bin gekumin zayen zeyen in der velt, says the holy man
I have come for this, I have come for that, says the Baal Shem Tov
but as for me I have come to tread in the brown tar of your cities
     and I have come to watch light glitter on automobile graveyards
I have come to kiss under beeches with bark of elephant skin
     and I have come to sob under elm wineglasses
I have come to worship reflections of traveling cumuli in architectural glass
     and I have come to adore the khaki blankets of homeless men
I have come to sniff dried blood in the newsprint
     and I have come to swim like a virus on electromagnetic ripples
I have come to pray like Hannah moving my lips sitting on asphalt
     and I have come to rave like Jonah in beery ballparks
I have come with my child to your hysterical stock exchanges
     and I have come with my grandchild to your hypocritical congresses
I have come to exchange curse for curse with the sanctimonious microphone
     and I have come to return your bronze medals
I have come in humility to beg and scratch in the dust
of your mass graves until you rise up
and I have come to defecate
in your chapels

until the death of the word "until"
I don't want you to be proven scientifically, I want you to appear
to me and to all peoples in your true form
of ruthless radiance

then

after that it snowed
a crispy inch or so
and after this the sky
resumed her rinsed blue scintillance

and after that I remembered the birds
so I filled the feeders with two kinds of seed
and after this a cardinal
a red-capped woodpecker

and some finches
have been flying around
Now you are smirking at me
See how simple it really is

to receive a blessing

~

We make each part perform multiple parts
and in that sense each of us is your poem:

the endocrine system immeasurably old
already estrogen appears in yeast

light sensitive cells may have evolved
among slow habitants of coral reefs

inexorably propelled by appetite
toward high bright tides teeming with diatoms

pores rimmed open for sweating blushing
skin itself a pouch

of wet organs transmitter of touch
the sly invader the baffling thief

What a piece of work is man
what an interminably dancing fount

and is it true you treasure us

3. mother

honor your mother
what if it commanded only that
honor your mother

against nature which
bids you flee her
honor while despising

while wrestling free
while avenging
this unasked for

gift of life

~

unasked for disappointing hateful life
it is the mother's fault

we fall from her space into the world
webs of organs helpless

what a pity she does not eat us
and be done with it

rats do
lions do

in dry times

4. descent

The year dives toward its close. There is something so glamorous in its descent. As the waves make toward the pebbled shore, our minutes hasten to their end. The gray-gold afternoon shudders down to indigo, transparent. It is full darkness by six.

Whoever is speaking or will speak in these pages, I welcome you. Let me be your vehicle. Let me be the mouth of your tunnel. Or the split in the earth.

5. psalm

I am not lyric any more
I will not play the harp
for your pleasure

I will not make a joyful
noise to you, neither
will I lament

for I know you drink
lamentation, too,
like wine

so I dully repeat
you hurt me
I hate you

I pull my eyes away from the hills
I will not kill for you
I will never love you again

unless you ask me

~

You have made everything wondrous after its kind
the x molecule hooks the y molecule

mountains rise with utmost gravity
snow upon their shoulders

a congress of crows circulates through the maize
that grows sheeny through a breezeless morning

the ribbed leaf a spot of scarlet floats
on the shivering creek

each single thing so excellent in form and action
whether by chance by excitement by intention

you draw along a dappled path the wren
to her nest, the fledglings cry, the lions flow

rhythmically toward the antelope, the butterfly
flicks yellow wings, the galaxies

propagate light in boundless curves
past what exists as matter, as dust

You have done enough, engineer
how dare we ask you for justice

~

Do not think I fail to remember

you were right there
clasping me
when we danced
without words
commandments
fear
oh it was so good
oh it was like melting
oh it was like a rainbow
so where in hell
are you now

you can tell I'm lonely

the red thread

The extended lines of relations meet. . . .
Every particular Thou is a glimpse through to
the eternal Thou.

—Buber, *I and Thou*

1. the red thread

the barren wife wraps it around a stone
seven times, her womb
burns for a son

a priest drapes it across
his comfortable belly, a surgeon
clamps it and snips

the disturbing red thread
invisible yet warm
travels between earth and heaven

vibrates through starless void
razon, oh will of God, *your will be done—*
only this red thread is so thin

pull it through
your fingers, a chill
ripples your skin

does it carry the pulse
of our prayers
like a bulge in a snake

dozing, like a stream
of hungry bloody hope, do all
the red threads join

form a web

2. mother

> The commandment to honor our parents is the
> hardest of all. But only then will our relationships
> with those around us be transparent to us. And only
> then will our desire to be good be within our reach.
>
> —Lawrence Kushner

although I have put an ocean between us
still do you know how I lie awake at night
the eye in my right palm pictures you
sitting amid your litter, feet buried
by accumulated jars of buttons,
glasses lost beneath a decade of bank statements
and funny poems,
hands folded under your chin, staring
at nothing, preparing to be blind
and helpless, for fifty years
it has tortured me that I cannot save you from madness
and that I do not love you enough

what is enough
nothing is enough

~

desert

you are fond of explosions
let me tell you
no explosion is necessary
another way to arrive at death
is by deforestation

people, you know, are like ants
relentless
bite whatever they need

it is a slow death
it takes centuries
while my curved and folded flanks adorned by pelts
become denuded useless
my canopy consumed

the tribes drift away then
perhaps leaving some broken axes behind
or some designs carved into stone

they who were so in need of fire

⁓

waste

secretly, someone called *he* is behind it all
the absent mathematician
the endless one
or so they say
those who believe in logic and reason
a world of equations where nothing is wasted

it may be as they suppose

what I find in the foreground is you
monologist, mistress of futility
seething through cycles of fat and thin
nervously sorting changeless debris
rags, furniture, rotted steaks
killing and saving, more or less at random,
beetles, roaches, flies,
writing illegible puzzles
dead fish crammed in your ceiling

~

now you dare

you always wanted *me* to be *your* mother
now you do it by supposed accident

you dare to call me your mother
I who am merely your irresponsible daughter
without shame you exhibit your toothless face
blindness and helplessness
selfishness memory loss
stinking incontinence
whether I wish or not
it is you, isn't it
I must cherish
mama
maya
even if winter sleet assaults the windows
like urine, hisses *too late, too late*
I myself must decide it's not too late.

~

mom, reach into
your barrel of scum-coated blessings.
find me one.

3. dialogue

> When you harmonize bitter enemies
> yet resentment is sure to linger.
> How can this be called good?
>
> —Lao Tzu

I tried to invent new forms of holiness
to console myself
after the event at the mountain
Behold I put before you
life and death therefore
choose life, I said
but look at you
look at the stiffness of your neck
look at the desire of your heart
to wreck everything

with your harlotry

～

I am named *k'dsha*, harlot, whore, abomination
while you are named *kaddosh*, holy, separate or apart

terrified of the gulf into which we blindly reach
do I not seek your face, you mine

attempting to touch we destroy we break we are broken
yet do we not share a root   a thread   dear friend

～

I said Let us reason together, I said I hate your sacrifices, I said feed the hungry
I said clothe the naked, I said do justice, love mercy, I said keep my law

～

dear one

I believe someday we will show each other our bruises
after this dialogue of the deaf

but tell me, where it is written
I found you in your blood, and I said, Live,
who speaks to whom
who forgives whom

the shekhinah as exile

hidden one: when the temple fell
when Jerusalem arose and fell and whenever
we were persecuted and scattered
by the nations,
to follow us in pain in exile
you folded wings patched coats
dragged mattresses pans in peasant carts, lived your life
laboring praying and giving birth, you also
swam across the hard Atlantic
landed in the golden land
they called you greenhorn
you danced in cafes
you went in the factory
bargained pushcart goods ice shoes Hester Street
put on makeup threw away wigs
and you learned new languages
now you speak everything
lady, but part of you is earth
part of you is wounds
part of you is words
and part is smoke
because whoever was burned over there, you were burned
you died forever with the sheep
whoever survived, you speak in our tongues
open your wings, instruct us
say what we are
do not confuse us
with the sanhedrin of the loud speakers
who have no ear for your voice
but we who thirst for your new
instructions, source of life
come into our thoughts

our mouth. Speak to us
voice of the beloved

help us
say what we are
say what we are to do

4. the red thread again

this night
I dreamed a dream
I do not understand it

stretched from earth
to heaven from heaven
to earth this red thread

my entrails drawn
shamelessly from my body
too much and too far

save me save me

~

—*for Feroza Jussawalla, in exile*

fathers explain to children
you will wear these threads
to protect yourselves
and for purity

ten thousand Parsis fleeing Muslims
thread round their waists
knotted front and back
run to India

ten thousand grandfathers
by fringes and by straps swaying
hoping to be tethered and the red
thread floats in the void

a sign a sign
you have to smile
as if you were going to protect them
and as if purity helped

so many favorite children, isn't it
a kind of orphanage

5. riddles

when I try to look into my soul
something always interrupts
like a stone dropped into a well

what is this foolish fear in my stomach
turning like a wheel
Is it that mother will be angry

that the universe will forget me
that the soul will be empty
or like a broken jar

~

answers

when the mother is dancing
and everybody is worshiping her
then she doesn't punish

a wind blows through the universe
causing forgetfulness
they say
the best soul is the most empty
the most broken

~

some hard traveling

one thing at a time
one foot in front of the other
city to city and every millennium
evacuated to the next
where are you
god
it's a damn long journey

~

god
been gone so long
why don't you call

~

can't remember why we separated
was it you who wanted freedom
was it me

~

the secret

the secret shape of this book is a parachute
all the lines leading to the person hanging there

drifting on the wind and always falling
waiting for the mists to clear

III ∼   february–march 1999

deaths, transfigurations

And he said unto me, son of man, can these
bones live? And I answered, O Lord God,
thou knowest.

—Ezekiel 37.3

i. fire

the Lord your God is a consuming fire

the stories of the gods outshine the moon
your story is darkness outshining the sun

we hide our eyes because of your fire
at the moment of the mountain

let not God speak to us lest we die

~

no wonder history gives us
cities like widows
sitting in their menstrual blood

no wonder book of revelation surges up
four horsemen orgy of vengeance
after nonviolent gospels

no wonder swarms Christian soldiers
burning libraries
heretics

no wonder chapel in Cuzco
San Antonio striding upon
the prone body of an Indian

no wonder imams cut hands off sinners
no wonder the Jewish lunatic murders worshipers
in a place of reconciliation

everybody trying to look goes blind

~

One of these days
oh one of these days
will be a festival and a judgment

and our enemies will be thrown
into the pit while we rejoice
and sing hymns

Some people actually think this way

~

On a good day

there is a bridge that spans the flood
of spacetime pouring between
your imperial palace and our poor tenements

your domain, *ha-makom,* of purest
illumination
and our humble lives

to what can we compare your word
beloved it is like flying sparks
running through the four worlds

toward us, the reality cascades
to intellect to feeling
to flesh

like a long distance call
then we send the return message

blessed be you
blessed be you
what delight between you and us

⁓

the rest of the time
what
gnashing of teeth

what slamming doors

⁓

the yearning

> Not until the lower world
> was made perfect was the other world also made
> perfect. . . . and it is thus the yearning from below
> which brings about the completion above.
> —The Zohar

and so I am reading the zohar
and they are so splendid these old rabbis in their splendor
and their words are blazing light sparks gushing springs
and their hopes are palaces pomegranate trees perfumes ascending

glorious
but as for me
their gates stand closed
fastened against me

what must I do outside here
shake the latches and wail, they are deaf
mount a lawsuit against them, they are expert lawyers
scratch my scabs go on a hunger strike

forget it they own the cameras, oh my beloved
how long before you tell them who I am

2. blood

Of all bodily fluids, blood is the one most often named, the bravest
and most dramatic, the fluid of heroes and of atonement. The fluid
of crime. Of shame, when its river floods from a woman's body. It is
vivid red, and soon becomes clotted, sticky, stale. The tangy scent of it
is a stimulant. Simple people know this. Children dare each other to
taste it.

~

we are connected to earth by our menstrual blood
and the blood of warriors flowing from open wounds
like open lips, gratifying the soil
moistening dry bones—
without these things, can the earth yield?

3. earth: the shekhinah as amnesiac

> I was set up from everlasting, from the beginning
> before the earth was. . . . When he prepared the heavens
> I was there. . . . rejoicing always before him
>
> —Proverbs 8:23–30

then humanity named you wisdom
monarchs ruled according to your counsel
you prepared a table from which we ate

you were above rubies
and exalted like the palm tree
or like the rosebushes in Jericho

come on, surely by now you remember who you are
you're my mother my sisters my daughter
you're me

we will have to struggle so hard
to birth you
this time

the brain like a cervix

~

ritual, see Sanskrit *rŭt*, blood; *ṛtu*, time appointed for worship

it is said God spoke and the world came into being
now listen to this
holy one

a woman squats in a field
wheat stubble pricks her feet
smell of clods billows up

foggy middle of winter
air damp she shivers
she bleeds it helps the birth

of whatever means to be born

⁓

ten thousand years later

a woman writhes on a straw mat they can't hold her
digs nails into palms against the contractions

the instinct to cancel imposed anguish with chosen anguish
brow drowned in sweat the sun paralyzed

she lashes out at the midwives
why does nobody push the sun forward

⁓

another ten thousand

a woman in a ward
bed rubber pad   tubes
everywhere bleeds
through the green cotton
nightgown   the sheet sops

⁓

crown

they are only after power
the unborn heads they are like
battering rams inside it is
global war the unborn
pitted against everyone
until they crown

themselves
their holy
little faces

⁓

a woman

sun warm on her back
she is rocking back
and forth now

everyone who sees her laughs

hold on hold on push
now is the time
somebody catch the child

4. time

—for my husband

all this time
the arrow of desire

then the child is born
wet

and spills over into grandchild
spoon after spoon

snow falls on pines
rain on graves

see what happiness
when one speaks

up—up—a particular
dusty sunlit disorder

just what was intended
all this time

~

inflationary universe

as the needle reaches through a loop
pulls something from the other side through

this becomes the next loop
while the first one tightens

~

I blow in the baby's face

stirring the soft hair
over her forehead
she laughs blows back
in my eyes

IV ～   march–april 1999

covenant

In every generation each of us is obligated to
see ourselves as if we left Egypt.

—The Haggadah

1. preparing for passover

doors flung open
bread tossed to the birds
we shop for the matzoh the bitter
herbs the honey the eggs
the wine the brisket
the onions the potatoes
the escape the memory
of the escape

from what
to what
for what

promise

~

we remember blood midnight
so much blood smeared
and then and then

we were like sheep running
we had no knowledge
only fear
the dust in a haze
along our track
away from the cities
the man like a great dog
the flame pillar
the cloud pillar
terrifying
our baaing

when we saw the chariots
we started stampeding
toward the sea my god
you swept us
there you
hurled us across
like a wind raised
cliffs of water
far above us
oh yes we ran
track over track in mud
we got over
then the engorged water
folded like a scroll
over our enemies
when we understood they were dead
how we laughed how we danced

because you chose us you loved us
with our frightened sheep eyes
hysterical bleating
you watched us from
your fiery whirl
preparing laws to
change us from slaves
make us a free
nation your
instrument

you did not understand we were animals

now you drive us through the desert in circles
you send this man who herds us
you speak to him mouth to mouth
you do not speak to us

or you speak in riddles
though we beg you
though we dance
and sing for you

freedom

how it has to come from suffering

interlude: the song of Joshua

the inhabitants of Jericho
faint with fear
only the harlot
hangs the red thread

from her window
and is saved
with all her family
everyone else dies by the edge of the sword

you who accomplish this with a mighty arm
our mouths declare your praise
you plant us in the land

promise of figs and olives grapes and men
we have slain innocence
let history begin

2. during the bombing of Kosovo

hevel   may be translated vanity
or mist or vapor

it is evening it is morning one day
like mist from ten thousand feet
above the hills bombs fall
like vapor the thin air
is full of them
roads crawl with tanks soldiers
like mist tens of thousands
of refugees cross the border
like vapor from morning to dusk
unmanned families
like mist women in slippers
children in bare feet
like vapor carrying blankets
suitcases of clothes
like mist money
ripped off by border guards

not new under the sun
not new on throbbing bluelit screen
but the eye tires of seeing
the ear of hearing
oh we still prepare our feast
of liberty and memory
we remain your children

and you, you—
father of rain
what are you thinking

~

the spot of black paint
in the gallon of white
makes it whiter

so the evil impulse
is part of you
for a reason

what reason

greater wilder holiness

~

so perhaps you want us to understand
it throbs also in you
like leavening

you want us to love that about you
even if you pray that your attribute of mercy
may overcome your attribute of wrath

you want us always to love the evil also
the death-wish also
the bread of hate

because we are your image
confess you prize
the cruel theater of it

3. question and answer

the love of suffering
the suffering of love
that too is a spectacle to you
or do you feel it too
God, do you
feel it too

have you not guessed
your desire is mine your pain is mine

when the least portion of you suffers I curl
wincing into myself like a sea urchin

a woman in hard labor
or a stricken ox, have you not been told

the infected wound of your love inflames me
let me alone I will weep bitterly

what is worse than the contemptuous glance
of one to whom you have given your soul

4. the wheel

of history
of revelation revolution
shake rattle roll
spin it then

once in a lifetime
once a generation
you take to the street the meeting hall
the republic freedom brotherhood

you meet at the river where they sing

arise you prisoners of starvation
arise you slaves no more in thrall
which side are you on, gonna lay down
my sword and shield

doors slide open
the sheer heavens are telling
the glory of god the leaden
despotisms crashing

in the imagination
where a whole cosmos pulsates in delight
workers and students rulers and ruled
the fluent glance linked arms liberated hair

the decent wage the honest handclasp

big wheel turns doors smoothly re-lock
(the war is on again)
space capsule sealed your screen
illumines your eerie virtual world

remember the days of your youth
dogs police ranged against you
remember your tinted clay beads your quick soft lips
your sandals forever after

printed on the Mississippi tar

~

songs of innocence and of experience

> There is a fountain in a sacred deed
> —Abraham Joshua Heschel

A fine freedom a thrill
flows up our vertebrae
when we demonstrate
for peace for civil rights to save
the bluegreen planet, when we cross
the line, some call it *shakti,* some
call it *shekhinah,* some say
spiritus

Imagine a stream rippling
under crackling ice glaze
on a chilly march morning
imagine stiff curled leaves acorns
branches frozen in snowdrifts
imagine sap rising in maples, wet granite
boulders starting to dry
a bear meandering partially awake
stumbles over a downed branch
squirrels leap chitter
imagine the scent

Some call it the endocrine system,
rapture in the adrenals is the
reward of goodness, like sex
or eating it
pours all the way through
the libido the ego the superego—
we feel alive then

So do the thief, the liar,
the killer, the conqueror,
the enraged—
envious as a black hole—

tiger, lamb, tiger
raccoon—

we are that mixed animal
you are that mixed god

the mother

Do I move toward form? do I use all my fears?
—Muriel Rukeyser

1. eyesight

please, *please*
I can't see well
reassure me with your touch

or a tender word
the shade of a wing
just *one* jay feather

or snail shell, please visit me
listen to the story
of my life—

—and the rhododendrons arrive and so
you've survived another winter
shaky through clotted retinas

cruelly reduced to one or two chopped letters
at a time mother you have spent
a lifetime reading only

to learn what words cannot accomplish
though when I phone
today you say

there was so much sun
you sat outside
you could read again

～

the next day

bright sunshine, wind, life
flaring up in the street

dirt exhales grass
treetops wave foliage ruffles

like dancers then
shady lower boughs lift

the maples appear to be waltzing
at the chlorophyll ball

then mother when I call you say
you tried going out
even with a coat
there was too much wind

too much
wind

~

the day after

you remind me you were a wild one
you used to beat up the boys on your block

you were teacher's pet, you won prizes for poetry
you had beautiful eyes

you tell your neighbor I am your moon and stars
you are upset the plumber stole your purse

so I drive over and find it
on the counter among the flies

2. our mothers: a correspondence

—*for Toi Derricotte*

I send you my whitehaired poems
you reply: *our small box of words*
if we were men we would call it a word-hoard
like the warriors and bards in Beowulf

if we were real men
we would strut not cringe
over our language
what would we do
if we were real women

feed the hunger
chew everything
use up the words in the box
before we die
leave nothing to rot

~

mother you coldly remark
as if with curled lip *some women*
walk away over the ice
leave their old mothers
to the wolves
in times of poor fishing
or when we cannot
bear them on our backs
any further

the wolves pace
just outside the perimeter of firelight
we can hear them pant
we know the muscled grace
of their gray bodies all night in motion

~

all poetry is, you say,

              an attempt
to name the disappearance
that got in the way—
and I rise from my chair thinking yes,

it's the goddess, let's face it—
when they chopped her groves down
nailed her shrines shut
forgot the words to her songs

when she stalked back to myth
we lost something worth having
the men did it but the women
cooperated as usual

then there were ages
when stones dropped from walls
cities disappeared from the light of heaven
scattered buried

some statues remained
some painted figurines, some clay icons
snakes writhe in their fists
behind museum glass

we need to blame someone
we scream at our mothers
where is she? what have you
done with her?

~

the shekhinah as mute

our mothers tremble vibrate
hesitate at the edge of speech
as at an unmade bed, their mouths work, confused

our mothers helpless to tell us
She whom you seek sacrificed
her place before the throne

dived into the atomic structure
of matter and hides there
hair wings streaming

womb compassionate pitiless
eyes seeing to the ends of the universe
in which life struggles and delights in life

they cannot take our hands show us
how to take comfort in raisins and apples
break apart laughing spit seed

they cannot say *seek me*
they teach us cooking clothing craftiness
they tell us their own stories of power and shame

and even if it is she who speaks through their mouths
and has crawled through ten thousand wombs until this day
we cannot listen

their words fall like spilled face powder

~

learn to recognize the gestures

when her hands cup her breasts
she enjoys her sweet strength
sap ascends the oak

dancing she causes
the young to dance
and to kiss

she may carry a weapon
a knife a gun a razor
she may wear a belt of skulls

when she discharges her anger in laughter
white lightning illuminates the horizon
from pole to pole

often she lays her hand over her eyes
like a secretary leaving
an office building at evening

cradling that infant boy
sitting him on her lap
smoothing the folds of her dress: this means pity

arms crossed: this signifies judgment

illusion

Have you not thought, O dreamer, that it may
be all maya, illusion?

—Walt Whitman

i. cinema

what if illusion and truth fuse, if we have sutured that wound
and if the film before our eyes is holy

we are silent we drink sugared water we eat sweet fats
lift puffed corn to our lips and magnified and glorified

beauty fans across the wide white screen, your male and female beauty
we are dreaming their glamour they are dreaming our humility

we behold miracles the Red Sea parts, the cavalry thunders
down the canyon, the aircraft release dark pellets into a pale sky. . . .

how strange we are coiled here in utero
like pears in syrup, seeing pictures move . . . and moving. . . .

hitting the curves on a cliff road over the Pacific
heading through a loud mercantile city pedestrians flying

we rock to a stop in a brick warehouse the criminals
elude us but wait, in the shootout someone is wounded

now we are in bed skin like taffeta tumbled hair
kissing divinely coupling. . . .

a splash of blood a cleared blue sky
humankind cannot bear life without deities

2. Cretan interlude: Lasithi Plateau

your knees like heavy cobbles
in a town square where men sit outside
a cafe stretching the morning

your hand fills the entire sky
with a blue gauze

you created this caldera now full of windmills
we finish our lunch of olive and feta, we bike the flat dirt roads

mountain crests ringing the irrigated land like a signature
of your name—a bluegray zero

one of your many fists probably a meteor did this
all is verdant fertile now in rows

where earth loosens her dress
more of your signs

~

the clothing of the island is olive groves
trim vineyards, crags
sudden ruins

~

the secondary road finds a crest and clings to it
we gaze back over the Libyan Sea

we stop in a village on a hillside that drops away
to a wide valley where a woman on a donkey climbs up

a path goats spilling after
like the train of a wedding gown

fine dust-free air
fine emptiness

a plane tree up behind the church a spring
a stone trough with six faucets six lion heads

an old man in the noon square at the cliff-edge begs coins
a retarded boy with a tree limb plays horse

an old woman waters her vegetables
a man builds a second story on his house

fine emptiness
fine dust-free air

~

Knossos

we have dreamed of coming here
and here is this handful of stones like rolled
dice, olive trees like iron

older than Greece, it is our dead childhood
sun clamps down on it
once we were heroes we thought

if we followed the red thread bravely
through damp corridors through dust
cobwebs storerooms armories

to the hot womb of the labyrinth
we would find the brutal horned monster
the bull of the earth

who is your enemy or your twin
throat coughing volcanic smoke
we would steep our hands in its blood

we imagined the goddess
with her furled dress and her snakes
to whom we would kneel

today we learn it is impossible to unearth
what the hard clay surface buries
what time chooses to destroy

turn and return

I still have within me the lust to search for living water
with quiet talk to the rock or with frenzied blows.

—Yehuda Amichai

1. the poet in me says

I ask nothing for myself
for myself I don't care
if you exist it's material for art

if not—well,
it's the others I worry about
how will they live without you

though friends explain to me
Jews don't have to believe in god
for Jews, god is an option

and my friend Karen remembers
as a little girl
studying Hebrew she inquired

of her refugee tutor who stroked his beard
and said in Yiddish "if there is a god,
or if there isn't a god,

a Jew studies"—isn't that a good story
beloved, but the woman in me
says that the poet lies

the poet can afford to lie
the woman stuck in her eyeballs
handcuffed to the clock's injurious hand

only lives once
where are you damn you
beloved where are you

hiding this time, please come out
she keeps crying
she keeps looking

~

waterfall

the woman she is crazy everyone knows
she stands for craziness just before it goes over the
ribs of waterfall

spray filling the air the breeze represents
beauty born of despair, arm on the bar
the moment before the kiss

becomes more than social, the teeth
come into it, the tongue and teeth
as if returning to infancy

the galaxies fall toward us
burst away
every atom charged

God you know what it is
mostly it is all nothing
vapor   speed

to approach the divine
through the material
here I go

God I can't stop

like my ancestress, like you Bruriah
clear one of God
seduced

betrayed

here I go

~

Bruriah

—for Jane Schaberg

my ancestress
the one woman
who speaks in Talmud
an actual historical person
they say you learned
three hundred precepts from three hundred rabbis
in a single day a miraculous feat
they say when your sons died
you forestalled the grief of your husband
the great Rabbi Meir
saying: if someone lend me two jewels
then require them of me
what should I do
he said: return them
then you showed him the dead boys
and when your house was robbed
your husband wished to curse the thieves
so that they would die but you said
it would be better to pray
for their repentance
and they say once when Rabbi Jose
the conservative
met you on the road and
asked directions of you
you spoke to him ironically:
should you not use fewer words
when speaking to a woman

eight hundred years after your death
the sage Rashi relates a tale
that your husband cited a tractate
saying "women are light-minded"
that you denied this
that he set his student to seduce you
that you resisted then succumbed
and hanged yourself
let me beg to doubt this
the Romans liked such tales
Dido immolates herself for love
Lucrece stabs herself for shame
of such deeds the nations create high art
but what kind of story is this for Jews
why didn't your husband hang himself
for shame

my friend Jane visits Tiberias
the grave of Meir is a magnet
for pilgrims but
where is the grave of Bruriah
she wanders streets puzzled
no citizen can tell her where
you lie rather they seem appalled
or angry at the query
nobody has a clue
Bruriah my ancestress
how when you taught Torah
your words rang like a harp
so diligent you were
such soul you had

2. days of awe

elul: psalm 27

we are told to say the following
every day for a month
in preparation for the days of awe:

you are my light my help
when I'm with you I'm not afraid
I want to live in your house

the enemies that chew my heart
the enemies that break my spine
I'm not afraid of them when I'm with you

all my life I have truly trusted you
save me from the liars
let me live in your house

~

rosh hashanah

the birthday of adam
the innocent earthling
and the day hagar and ishmael
found water in the desert

in memory of whom
mud staining our shoes
water flowing in handfuls
we sniff the smell of living dying things

reach into our pockets
for the bread that represents
our sins, toss it in, praying release
us, help us, forgive us

the river answers
by swallowing our crumbs

do our prayers travel upward
do they defy gravity
like rain splashed on the windshield
of a car speeding through storm

in ten days we will go hungrier
pray harder

~

yom kippur

we destroy we break we are broken
and this is the fast you have chosen
on rosh hashanah it is written
on yom kippur it is sealed

who shall live and who shall die
which goat will have his throat cut
like an unlucky isaac

spitting a red thread and which goat
will be sent alive to the pit where the crazies are
thread tied lightly around its neck

who will possess diamonds and pearls
and who will be killed
by an addicted lover

who shall voyage the web of the world
like an eagle, and who shall curl to sleep
over a steam grate like a worm

who shall be photographed and whose
face will disappear like smoke

this is the fast you have chosen, *turn return*
how to turn   like leaves   like a page   like a corner
what is our knowledge, what is our strength

I am like the stones people place on graves to make them a little heavier
such a stone says, in its oracular way, *don't come back,* or *return only as grass*
but it is tired of being a stone, it wishes to be open, it would like to be an egg

honeybees manufacture honey, a power station generates electricity
cotton plants extrude smooth fiber, and my cells secrete anger
my mind propagates envy, *but repentance, prayer and good deeds*

avert the stern decree, I am like a ramshackle house during a hurricane
struck by guilt waves and fear waves, the walls could collapse any time
but the foolish old woman who lives there refuses to leave

~

addendum to jonah

I am alone at the party
the gaiety
of the falsely repentant
is like a lidless eye
leers at me
like a golden desert sun

*it is not your task
to judge but to speak
you are my teeth my tongue
Oh I see that you are sweating
wait wait where you are
I will be back—
I will bring comfort*

~

I have stopped burning
I know that you are full of mercy
I agree that you are compassionate
I sit in the shadow of your affection
I gaze out at the desert
I see that it is a garden
it is a dream

Awake awake, Jonah. Awake and utter a song.

~

a dead gourd
one of your jokes

are you very angry
be serious
your heartbreak is not interesting
it is your rhetoric that beguiles me
I liked your performance at Nineveh
just as I liked your song by the waters of Babylon
your legal brief at Uz
I want you to praise me hotly but more than that
I want you to save the world
by any means necessary
your word against
mine

the volcano and the covenant

I am molten matter returned from the core of
the earth to tell you interior things—

—Anne Carson

1. the volcano breathes

coughs   coughs up

～

if the subconscious is a *geniza*   like Cairo synagogue   piled attic
          twelve jars a shepherd finds in a cave   papyrus crumbs

repository [place of repose in which to put/push/press/repress
                pinched   her moist red   disturbed
                rose there   her terebinth   grove misremembered but]

can't throw anything away
holy holy holy
holy god holy name holy demon same

the mind can't
throw anything holy away
let it stay let it be she let it wait

～

oh god
yours and ours
it hurts

pain is the pressure of what attempts to be ex-
pressed and cannot be, oh shit, oh baby

          anguished impression is pressure to

she told them at the lecture the naked [failures] fathers
          what do you guess your pain and suffering mean
[she looked from the podium] looked round the room seated they were pretending
          no no pain no suffering

not me insisted their eyebrows not my face I am
a commercial for normal/eyes away
only a few lashes flickered

~

dry crust in quiet flame ready now
your labor pains persist indefinite exacerbate until
oh dear god, maybe never [fear is your driver/your doctor]

oh god, yours and ours, how they hurt so
bring forth your uterine self? by yourself? is it time's nick? [time present
she so buried so erased so unlawful so forgot so swallowed

like wolf swallowing grandmother [the being
called] god the father swallowed god the mother,
the process required millennia
you swallowed her down the hatch

meanwhile in the text she kicks watch that

to "raise the sparks" is metaphor is   imagination is!
to speak the unspoken unspeakable   stems pierce asphalt
lava through split stone, heaving water dividing
razon, oh desire of god, your desire be done
let the waters break from the waters   fireflow rise

want to be a midwife to
pull it out to dream

words of the mouth meditations of the heart
from the source the desire
is to flow without cease

I do have a heavy burden
and cannot wait to put it down

~

to put it down is forbidden

2. psalm 37: the meek shall inherit the earth

try not to be angry
at the meanness of men, they fade like grass
in october, nothing of them remains

trust me to give you what you need
leave it to me, I will vindicate you
and give you whatever you want

the mean men will shoot themselves in the foot
all by themselves and even their children
will fail to thrive

the meek believed these promises
these deep whiffs of opium
once upon a time

while the arrogant went about their business
the words continued to be contrafactual
and very beautiful

they shall not hurt nor destroy
nation shall not lift up sword

3. I decide to call you Being

a word with two contradictory
meanings   someone to wipe the blood
and dirty tears away through boundless love

someone able to punish listen wrestle
like a person but
larger

and *ein sof*   boundless
being   in the sense of pure existence   remote
abstraction more impersonal than zero

you exquisite
joke   you paradigm paradox
you absent presence   you good evil   shredding the eye

so that it can become a door
you are inexplicable   like a *koan*
running uphill barefoot
blowing   the door down

      you complete nothing

      you perfect nothing

~

everyone asks   are you the father or the king
or the mother or the snake   but to me
listen you are the hope of my heart
you are the quarrel in my art

you are the tangled quarrel in my art
like a married pair who will go to their graves
carrying resentments like suitcases of foreign coins

you are the sex in my art
whatever wants to faint under long kisses, whatever grapples
flesh to flesh, the nipple that reaches, the tongue that spills

4. interlude: the avenue of the americas

Above the tongues of taxicabs, the horns and buyers
the teeth of buildings grin at each other, the institutions
of media medicine publishing fashion

know how to
bite through human flesh
like hinged aluminum traps chopping the necks

of beavers, or like logging rigs, those saws
that go through a hundred-year-old
redwood in about three minutes

take out a thousand acres
of virgin oregon forest
annually because loggers need jobs

intellectuals need the special sections
of the New York Times stacked
on driveways

each rosy dawn, the Japanese need
the splinters these pines and spruces
finally get turned into

everybody needs what they can get
and more. Yesterday walking
between fifty-third and fifty-second

on the avenue of the americas at twilight on my way
to a good restaurant with good friends I passed
three beggars wrapped in plastic. Why not say

beggars?
Why invent novelty phrases like "the homeless"
as if our situation were modern and special

instead of ancient and normal,
the problem of greed and selfishness?
The beggars turned toward me

I put money in the woman's cup
though I didn't like her facial sores
her drowned eyes bobbed to the surface

as if they believed for a second
something new was about to happen
but nothing was

so the eyes sank rapidly back
like crabs into sand, and sorrow
pressed into me like a hot iron

after which I hurried through the hurrying crowd
sky overhead primrose and lilac, skyscrapers
uncanny mirrors filled with cloud bouquets

to overtake my friends who had strolled ahead
chatting so as not to be embarrassed
by the sight of charity

the rotting odor of need

interlude: subway

at columbus circle a tall man a short squinty man
and a large woman storm the A train
bibles held high and talk about joy

God is good they say give yourself to Jesus
you know God loves you brother
I know it says my seatmate
when I was in vietnam I tried to tell my buddies

about Jesus, they said they didn't believe
but when we were under attack and men were dying
you know what? They were yelling *God*
he says to the short missionary

You better believe it. I sure do says the man and the subway rolls
the team moves on
and I am silent as a cloud and wishful

~

interlude: bus driver

do you know why the Lord made this world? she asks
I shake my head and look anticipatory
for his own *Glory!* she says. For his *glory!*

~

interlude: new england

gold magenta russet and bronze leaves
still deck the trees the wind is quickly stripping

a gust whisks a sackful of beech and maple leaves upward
they disperse and float for a while like lucky mystics

like the raggedy disciples of the Master of the Good Name
ascending into bliss with him one sabbath evening as it were in his wake

in a *shul* somewhere in Poland
something to tell the children and grandchildren

~

the volcano and the covenant

as if one could cut a covenant
with a roaring volcano

imagine our souls
being birthed and destroyed

the way a flame
uncurls in one instant

and when the next passes, it is no more
yet is like a scorching white word

in the red ongoing song
then gray ash that crumbles

softly to nothing, oh to
burn like that

5. toward the millennium

The coming winter's dark draws something in me. There is an "at last,"
a "finally" in the air, a transparency of soldierly gray days circling
toward peacock blue twilights, and into shelterless night. Spangles of
stars. Jupiter in the northeast a far fat pinhead of white fire.

In Central Africa boys of fourteen (I find myself thinking as my
husband and I take an after dinner walk on lamplit streets) pass
through villages scything the fingers and hands from women and
sometimes older men. Probably in the heat of the sun. Gold is too rich
for us.

The cold, the elimination of passion, the dark, the descending quest for
purity and truth. The air smells like an edge of snow, a front
approaching. A few nights ago the wind was wild, the trees were
raving, and the gale blew on into the next afternoon.

We were biking along Prospect Street in the gloaming on Saturday
night and the bare black boughs swept above our heads. The moon
hung in the air with her shadow. It was exciting but impossible to know
why.

A romantic memory of full summer foliage. Then the operatic autumn
in which one tree after another is transformed to a torch. In the end,
finally, and what a relief it is, rain peppers the leaves, wind rips them,
and they fall. The world shows itself to us in its mute truth. The arms
of the trees webbed and interlaced.

Far northwest of here, snowflakes have already begun to drift into a
yard. The snow underfoot is two feet deep. A man adjusts a buckle on
his husky's harness, pats the dog's thick black and white back. The dog
pants, his eyes are like large wet beads, his pink tongue is the most
vivid visible thing. The man rubs the husky between the ears, you feel
the pleasure. He gets into the sled and they go off into the whiteness.

~

does the dog lead or does the sled

who or what is sending me this image
earthling and animal heat
black figures in a white landscape,
small running figures
vast whiteness

~

and in the whiteness a speck
but god was not in the speck
then a soft wind
but god was not in the wind
then a breast and a great hand

6. predawn

ruach, ruach, the language to say it
ruach, ruach, wind, spirit, breath
spirit of god on the deep's face
spirit of god moved on the face
of the deep, spirit
moved

spirit was moving, spirit was moving
ruach elohim
the face of the deep waters moved
first it was dark darkness was on it
the face of the deep darkness was upon it
then the spirit came the wind came
the breath came and it moved

it moved, the breath came
and it moved
ruach it
moved

~

what did the stars do
the stars sang for joy
what did the hills do
they leaped like young rams

what does the day do
it tells the next day
what does the night do
whisper to the next night

what shall I do

the space of this dialogue

How the invisible
roils. I see it from here and then
I see it from here.

—Jorie Graham

1. psalm

I endure impure periods
when I cannot touch you

or even look at you
you are a storm I would be electrocuted

by your approach then I feel some sort of angelic laughter
like children behind a curtain

come, I think
you are at my fingertips my womb

you are the wild driver of my vehicle
the argument in my poem

nothing between us
only breath

~

psalm

> Oh green green willow oh wonderfully red flower
> but I know the colors are not there
> —Ikkyu

when I return to you
wet from the bath

throbbing through the change
from absence to presence

from the mask to the face
the honey eyes

crystal for complexity
and transparency

the sky transparent crystal
so my words

my life pure again through the rain
of impassioned phenomena

who cares how it happens

~

psalm

my head is uncovered to my naked hair
I am dressed immodestly

my old body lacks teeth, lacks a breast
still cherishes itself

I eat what I want I am
an animal of flesh

as you know for you formed me in the womb
and made my desires what they are

I am waiting for you
in a bed of pleasure

~

psalm

like a skin on milk
I write to you

I hurl the letters of your name
onto every page, one and many

I know you are reading over my shoulder
look each of us possesses a book of life

each attempts to read what the other has scripted
in these almost illegible letters tipped by crowns

what is the story
we want to know

~

would you turn off that faucet, I shout to my husband
but to you I say: never turn it off

2. seasonal

when the full sun is on me this way
I itch and am satisfied

I take it in like a thirsty man
swallowing water from his garden hose

I take it in like a smiling woman receiving
a curly-headed man, and then when the gilded leaves

rush past me sometimes I jubilate
like abraham I am here for this I came

like isaac I laugh trembling
well at least I am alive

and like jacob I think in the spirit world they can never
experience pleasure the way flesh can

the body making love
the body nursing a child

the body fighting
playing basketball

even when it sickens
nursing its lesions

it struggles to stay
it clings to its bars

everything else is theology and folly

⌒

mikvah

    —with thanks to Phyllis Berman

late afternoon the august sun reddens
its power to heal us or scorch us wanes
we women undress on the grass

like flying-home exiles we greet our bodies
clasping hands praying dropping our towels
we climb into the hot tub

cedar smell water spark
in threes we immerse ourselves
like jewels fallen overboard we create

tiny splashes then the water quiets
fear loosens like flakes of dead skin
grief rises like steam

we immerse further
then we emerge breathe again
we speak in low voices

you join us
with our wet hair
each shyly having left some prayer down there

in the tireless flowing
out we climb
like showered robins

3. dark smile

Just now coming downstairs after returning some books to a shelf and reading
a few pages of a friend's book, his piece on Jacob's wrestling, I was flooded with
love for this friend, and in my happiness halfway down the stairs I thought to
glance at my interior—
there, very faintly, was the claw of the shekhinah, probing; there too was her
dark smile.

~

when she comes it will not be from heaven, it will be up from the cunts and breasts

it will be from our insane sad fecund obscure mothers

it will be from our fat scrawny pious wild ancestresses their claws

their fur and their rags

~

memory

I wanted to forget that I drank your milk
I wanted to uncurl your grip
and forget your sour smell

your voice pursued me into the tunnel
I ran splashing through puddles
it grew darker

I am afraid of rats and of darkness in strange places
the echo of gongs faded
I was in this concrete pebbly tube

finally it was completely dark
and so dank no breeze
no glimmer even of steel track

but the odor of mud
old snakeskins
hair

about to sell your house

yard overrun with raspberries
canes across the front walk
I fill two quart containers

with plump red berries
eating as I go
scratches inscribe my arms

I have hired someone to cut it all down
after you leave so this is the last crop
the fruit delightfully tender to the fingers

to the tongue deliciously sweet and tart
you would like me to eat it all
leave nothing for the neighbors

I am your child
you want to do something for me
mother, I am sixty-two

at last able to speak the sentence
I love you—I say it
before getting into the car

~

physical examination

you sit on the examination table
white hair flying
telling your tale

I sit on the leatherette and chrome chair
over your shoulder I look at the degrees
the aluminum shelves

the kindly doctor moves his hand
you remove your cotton blouse
lay it aside you wear no brassiere

you reveal your breasts
with their brown aureolas
my mouth waters

~

rewind

in the communal dining room
many of the residents scream

one woman repeats *I'm good, I'm good*
many sit and say nothing at all

you write a poem calling them *wounded animals*
we move you to a better wing

you claim someone has stolen your bathing suit
you tell people you love them

you sit with your ear to the cassette player
listening to a biography of Eleanor Roosevelt

when you came you had forgotten how to cook
you were living on saltines

my mother my queen
now you gain weight

here is the photo of you dancing
that was in the newspaper

I saved your writing even the scraps
I saved the letters praising you as a teacher

today you have wet yourself you have soiled your underpants
I embrace you when I arrive and when I leave

~

memory

first dream I remember
maybe I was three
wearing a little coat
you were pushing a baby carriage
down the block away from me
you were running
my mother my queen
I was trying to catch you

4. aperture

to undo the folded lie
to change the laws of history
to be the trumpet of a prophecy

who planted this seed in our muddy minds
who put pencil and tablet in our hands
who turned on the microphone

started running the tape that repeats
write it, write it
make a fool of yourself

～

I see myself

as an aperture, words pass through, addressing/imagining/inventing
One, of whom nothing is known that is not words. I am pressing hard.
I am pressing down. It hurts so much. It does not hurt at all, it simply
flies. It is the effort to imagine what needs to be imagined. It is the
desperation to imagine what needs to be imagined by us, in order to
exist, and it wants, it wants to come into existence.

It cannot exist yet, something else exists that is not adequate, not at all
adequate, and it so needs to burst forth from that place. But it hurts, it
hurts.

What reaches? What answers? From time to time something does
answer. Like the surface tension in a cup of silence, trembling. What
do I imagine is happening?

～

it calls me

what I enjoy is when
it blows through me
music I cannot name

summoned by
the strong force
of the computer

sounding like a wild virtual horn
in another room
I run upstairs

happy now happy now that
I am its attachment or appendage
you got me

under the skin of my chest
not that I can locate really
where the waves sway

~

because the truth is
the perishing world exists
but then you see there is the eternal

center everywhere circumference nowhere
inside outside
and means to align the two

are available dearly beloved friends
trees animals kisses
cars computers drugs

music meditation or
the spite of war
open windows

and the divinity pours through
like hot sunlight
oh god the relief

the open secret drives through
crashes the barriers splinter
a ball of light waves

~

it makes me laugh
fifteen years or so ago I said
I was waiting for you in the kitchen

I thought you would fall through the ceiling
sometime when I was boiling rice for dinner
mute and friendly as a refrigerator

if you choose a silicon chip to drift
your thought toward my inner ear my fingers
my dear your will be done

for decades I swam in estrogen
children clung on my neck men swam into my body
what splashes we made according to your will

now I perceive you approach me from the future
humming like a superjet at ease
on the cyberskyway

oh you pillar of cloud you beam of shrieking light
electrons
flying like bugs toward a swallow's beak

after all I am not a stone
though I have been patient as one
and though

you also inhabit stones
you bring a future that is not my death
sailing in foamy waves through the blue screen

like my grandchild I will learn
to say hello to say ball
to say go up

~

coda

I want everyone to understand these lines
say nothing

~

sometimes the stories take you and fling you against a wall
sometimes you go right through the wall

glossary

Baal Shem Tov: "Master of the Good Name," peasant founder of the Hasidic movement in 18th century Poland

ein sof: Hebrew "without end," a kabbalistic name for God

Elul: in Hebrew calendar, late summer month preceding the High Holidays of Rosh Hashanah and Yom Kippur

geniza: in late antiquity and the middle ages, a storage place where unusable sacred documents (i.e., documents which named God) were kept to protect them against desecration or destruction

Haggadah: "The story," book used in Passover ritual, telling the story of the Israelite exodus from slavery in Egypt

ha-makom: from a Hebrew noun meaning "the place," a rabbinic name for God

koan: absurd question posed by a Zen master to a student, designed to elicit a response that transcends logic

mikvah: ritual bath used for spiritual purification

razon: will, desire

Rosh Hashanah: "head of the year," or new year; beginning of the High Holidays, or days of awe, a period of soul searching and repentance. It is a custom on this day to cast breadcrumbs representing one's sins into a body of flowing water

ruach: spirit, wind, breath; *ruach elohim:* spirit of God

shakti: Tantric equivalent of the Shekhinah, indwelling female energy, invoked in kundalini yoga

Shekhinah: from a Hebrew noun meaning "dwelling;" the presence of God on earth and/or the feminine aspect or emanation of God; in kabbala, seen as the object of devotional prayer and meditation; said to have been divided from God at the moment of creation, and to be yearning for reunion; said to have entered exile with her people after the destruction of the second temple in 70 C.E.

shul: house of prayer, house of study

Talmud: vast rabbinic compendium of Jewish law, folklore, midrash and philosophy; the Babylonian Talmud, compiled in the 6th century C.E., remains authoritative for Orthodox Jews throughout the world

Yom Kippur: "Day of Repentance," final day of the High Holidays, a day of collective prayer and turning to God, in which destinies are sealed in the heavenly Book of Life for the coming year

Zohar: "Book of Splendor," 14th century kabbalistic work; most important literary document in Jewish mysticism

acknowledgments

Thanks to the following publications, in which some of the poems in this collection first appeared, some in earlier versions or with different titles:

Alaska Quarterly Review, American Poetry Review, Cross/Currents vol. 49, no. 4, winter 1999/2000, *5 A.M., The Forward, Gettysburg Review, Judaism, Long Shot, Nimrod, Poetry/Flash, Prairie Schooner, Princeton University Library Chronicle, The Progressive, Seneca Review, Spoon River Poetry Review, Tikkun,* and *Women's Review of Books.*

I wish also to express my thanks to the MacDowell Colony and to the Bellagio Study and Conference Center for residencies which enabled me to work and play with these words.

Alicia Suskin Ostriker is a poet and critic whose previous volumes of poetry include *The Imaginary Lover* (1986), which won the William Carlos Williams Award of the Poetry Society of America, *The Crack in Everything* (1996), which was a National Book Award finalist and won both the Paterson Poetry Award and the San Francisco State Poetry Center Award, and *The Little Space, Poems Selected and New 1968–1998*, also a National Book Award finalist. Her critical works include *Stealing the Language: The Emergence of Women's Poetry in America* (1986), *The Nakedness of the Fathers: Biblical Visions and Revisions* (1994), and *Dancing at the Devil's Party: Essays on Poetry, Politics, and the Erotic* (2000).